The History of Education
on the Old Mission Peninsula

By Karen Rieser

KDP
Printed in the U.S.A

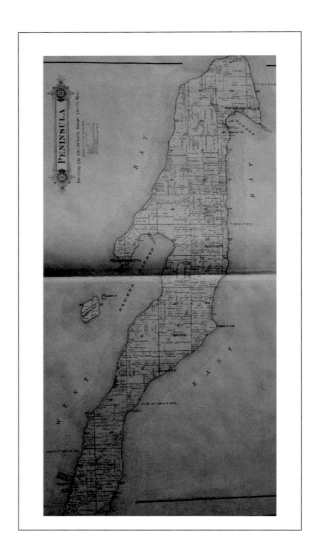

Map of the seven Old Mission Peninsula school districts in 1880.
Platt Map of 1890

Dedication

Written in honor of all the children and adults, past, present, and future, who have kept or will keep alive the possibility of acquiring a high-quality education on the Old Mission Peninsula.

Old Mission Peninsula Elementary School presents a holiday concert to the Old Mission Peninsula Historical Society on December 7, 2017. Photo courtesy of Christopher Rieser.

Acknowledgements

Learning is as much a part of life as breathing, eating, and growing. When do we begin to learn? Miraculously, the journey begins as soon as the brain begins to develop a cell or two. In the womb, the fetus learns to move, recognizes warmth, and attaches the idea of safety to the sound of its mother's heartbeat. For the remainder of our lives, we learn. Our survival requires it.

The History of Education on the Old Mission Peninsula traces the evolution of education from the peninsula's first inhabitants, the Anishinaabek, who resided here in the mid 1700s, to the fledgling charter school, Old Mission Peninsula School, that opened in September of 2018.

As I wrote, I became both teacher and student. As teacher, my formal education kicked in as I researched and pulled information from my general knowledge base. I became the student as I interviewed individuals with advanced knowledge and experience in a variety of areas.

I would like to thank Isadore Toulouse, tribal elder of the Little Traverse Bay Bands of Odawa Indians, for teaching me about Native American education and culture.

JoAnn and Bill Cole, thank you for providing information on Reverend Peter Dougherty and the genesis of the original mission and school.

I would also like to thank Marty Klein for telling me the story of the *Madeline*.

Jerry Ostlund, Tim Carroll, and Calvin Jameson, thank you for sharing your experiences in the one-room schoolhouses.

I would like to express additional thanks to Tim Carroll for providing the 1880 map of the seven former Old Mission Peninsula school districts.

Thank you to Christopher Rieser for your time and the many photographs you provided that are sprinkled throughout the book.

Jack and Vi Solomonson and Mary Jo Lance, thank you for allowing me to use photographs from your marvelous book, *A Century of Service: The People and Places on Old Mission Peninsula*.

Thank you to Horizon Books for allowing me to use the dashing picture of Chief Aghossa from *100 Years from the Old Mission: A Century in Grand Traverse County*.

Finally, thank you to the Hartley family for allowing me to use the picture of your beautiful children as representatives of the new Old Mission Peninsula School that opened in September 2018.

Table of Contents

Introduction

Education

The bee is a perfect symbol of education. Its purpose is to sustain life by pollinating the flora on which our very existence depends. Every plant presents a unique blossom that requires the bee to adjust its approach to attain its goal. In addition, the bee is challenged by numerous outside factors such as insecticides, loss of habitat, viruses, and as yet unforeseen events. Thus far, the bee has survived due to science, education, and concern.

The journey of the bee is similar to the journey of education. Our ability to survive is in direct correlation to our level of education (the bee). Educators have had to adjust their approach over the centuries as lifestyles and the requirements of survival have changed. Outside factors such as cultural shifts, technology, and politics continue to challenge our educational model, yet here on the Old Mission Peninsula, education continues to thrive.

What exactly is education? Although I've spent the majority of my life as either a student or educator, I still ponder the question. While brainstorming, I sought a list of synonyms. Some of the more pleasing were these: culture, improvement, scholarship, apprenticeship, civilization, guidance, enlightenment, coaching, nurture, and preparation. I also identified some disturbing and bewildering words: discipline, training, brainwashing, breeding, and drilling.

The multidimensional reality of education is well represented by these synonyms. The fact that the idea of education is so varied might also explain some of the heat that emanates from political discussions concerning its implementation. Therefore, before continuing with this work, the concept of education must be defined.

The noun "education" is said to represent "the act or process of imparting or acquiring general knowledge, developing the powers of reasoning and judgment, and generally of preparing oneself or others intellectually for mature life." That sounds great, yet education is not a concept that exists in isolation. Education is affected by outside factors such as life requirements, social conditions, politics, and location and cannot be discussed without taking these factors into account.

Education is delivered both formally and informally. Informally, we learn by living, observing our actions, analyzing the consequences, and changing or maintaining our behavior. Formally, we receive clearly defined information delivered in a purposeful and organized manner. As the human experience evolves, so do the methods of education.

For the purposes of this book, education is defined as both the formal and informal presentation of knowledge leading to the ability to reason and judge so as to enable the learner to survive and prosper as an adult. Turn the pages and see for yourself how and why education has evolved into what it is today.

Chapter One

Location, Location, Location

The Old Mission Peninsula is often called a paradise, and indeed it is, with its fertile soil, hardwood trees, fresh water, sandy beaches, and an abundance of fish and wildlife.

As part of the Great Lakes system, the peninsula was formed during the Wisconsin glacial period more than ten thousand years ago when immense mile-thick sheets of ice carved basins that began collecting meltwater. The glaciers gouged the Earth's surface, leaving irregular land configurations, and the higher land levels became islands and peninsulas. The Old Mission Peninsula is the result of this uneven erosion.

Running eighteen miles north of Traverse City, the peninsula divides Grand Traverse Bay into east and west arms and terminates at Mission Point where the historic lighthouse is located. The tip of the peninsula lies on the 45th parallel, or halfway between the North Pole and the equator. Fifteen miles northwest of Mission Point, Grand Traverse Bay becomes Lake Michigan.

Over nearly two centuries, the people who found their way to the Old Mission Peninsula lived a predominately agricultural lifestyle. The first orchard in northwest lower Michigan was planted on the peninsula, and farms today continue to yield world-class crops of cherries, apples, grapes, and more. This extraordinarily unique place in the heart of Michigan's fruit belt benefits year-round from the moderating effects of the water surrounding it.

Crops on the peninsula thrive in part because Grand Traverse Bay regulates the air temperature throughout the year. Winds moving over chilled winter waters lower the air temperature, delaying spring budding and making summers cooler, while winds passing over summer-warmed waters increase winter air temperatures, delaying frost, extending the growing season, and eliminating many killer freezes.

To fully understand education on this marvelous peninsula, we must look to the people who have made it their home. Our journey begins with the Native American peoples, the Anishinaabek, then moves to the *Madeline*, a maritime school. Next, we will visit the Peter Dougherty era, then move on to the one-room schoolhouses and the consolidated school. We will conclude with a charter school that, today, is a fledgling endeavor nourished by the rich and unique setting that is the Old Mission Peninsula.

Cherry blossoms on the Old Mission Peninsula.
Photo courtesy of Christopher Rieser.

References

Geocaching.com, Old Mission Peninsula.

Traverse City Environmental Stewardship Assessment 2012, Old Mission Peninsula.
Traversecitymi.gov.

Chapter Two
Education and the Odawa and Ojibwa Tribes

The Little Traverse Bay Band of Odawa (Ottawa) was the first Native American tribe to settle in the Grand Traverse area. The band includes the Odawa, Ojibwa (Chippewa), and Bodowadomi (Potawatomi) tribes.

Oral history reports that the eastern coast of Turtle Island, also known as Canada and North America, was the birthplace of the Odawa. Spiritual leaders advised the tribe to travel west until it found food growing in the water. During its travels, the tribe found wild rice growing in the waters on the Manitoulin Islands of northern Lake Huron. In the 1400s, the Odawa people called these islands home. To this day, they consider this their place of origin.

In the 1630s, the Odawa began to settle in Mackinac, or Upper Michigan. Attacks by the Iroquois in 1651 sent the tribe to Green Bay, Wisconsin. Later, in 1658, the Odawa migrated to the south shore of Lake Superior. Eventually, when the French drove the Iroquois out of the Great Lakes region, the Odawa returned. Some settled in Mackinac while others moved further south and east.

It was the failure of the soil in Mackinac that prompted the Odawa to migrate to the Grand Traverse region in 1741. Several tribes chose to settle on the Old Mission Peninsula in what is now the village of Old Mission. During the spring, summer, and fall, Old Mission was their home. They sought warmer regions to the south during the winter months.

Education for the Odawa people was a matter of cultural and physical survival. At its core was the belief that community is more important than the wishes of the individual. Maintaining and perpetuating this belief required educating one and all.

Native American education, delivered by the community on a daily basis through everyday life, conveyed knowledge, values, skills, attitudes, and dispositions to the youth. Learning was based on respect for nature and the human responsibility to learn and care for it (Yeboah).

The primary educators were grandparents. After the age of six, children were taught by adults in gender specific groups. Birchbark scrolls recorded information important to the tribe. The final teachings came through oral history or storytelling.

The wigwam, a cone-shaped windowless structure covered with sheets of birchbark and mats, was the home of the extended Native American family. It was possible for twenty or thirty family members to share a wigwam. Within the extended family, there could be multiple sets of grandparents.

By its very definition, "grandparent" suggests years of experience resulting in great wisdom, patience, and time for family. "Grandparents taught the children while the parents were making life happen," explains Pat Putney, elder/cultural department manager of the Grand Traverse Band of Ottawa and Chippewa Indians.

Boys and girls were both educated. After the age of six, boys followed male family members and girls accompanied female family members as they "made life happen." Fathers, male elders, uncles, and grandfathers taught the boys to hunt, fish, fight, and make weapons. Mothers, aunts, female elders, and grandmothers taught the girls to tend the gardens, weave baskets, sew, and gather fruits, herbs, and medicines. The boys and girls came together to cook, which was a shared responsibility.

The story called "The Three Sisters" imparted an important lesson to Native American girls. According to legend, corn, beans, and squash were inseparable sisters given as gifts from the Great Spirit to provide a healthy diet and keep the soil fertile.

The first step in creating a Three Sisters garden was to know when to begin planting. Nature would reveal the proper time—either when the Canada geese returned, or the dogwood leaves were the size of a squirrel's ear. The next step was to create a mound. If the soil was poor, bury several rotten fish or eel as fertilizer, then begin planting.

Corn, the oldest sister, went in the ground first. After it grew several inches, it was time to plant the beans, the third sister, at the base of the corn. Squash, the second sister, was planted at the edge of the mound. Finally, a seldom-mentioned fourth sister, beeweed, was planted among the plants to attract bees.

Each sister had a job. The corn provided support for the beans while adding carbohydrates to the diet. The beans, packed with protein, added nitrogen to the soil, keeping it fertile. The flesh and seeds of the squash provided vitamins and oil while its shallow roots and leaves mulched and shaded the soil, preventing water loss. The Three Sisters garden is still promoted today as "companion gardening."

Fish, including suckers, catfish, sunfish, salmon, and whitefish, the most popular, were the mainstay of the Odawa diet and necessary for survival. For the most part, fishing was a man's job. Four fishing techniques were passed on to young boys.

The first method required a gill net and could yield two hundred fish a night. Girls were taught to knit the nets out of natural fibers that included basswood and nettles. Boys learned how to carve the cedar floats and make holes in stones to be used as sinkers. Both boys and girls learned to set the nets.

Native American boys were also taught to use dip nets from canoes. This technique required two people, one in the bow to handle the net and one in the stern to paddle the canoe in a backward drift. Several large fish could be caught in each dip. When the canoe was filled with fish, the haul was taken ashore to be eaten, smoked, or dried.

Spears were also used for fishing. Boys were taught how to make the spears, their bone or horn points, and the torches required for spear fishing. Spear fishing happened at night or through the ice. Once the canoes were in deep water, the torches were lit. The fish, attracted to the light, were easily speared, but this method took a great deal of practice since water bends light, making the fish look closer than they are.

In the winter, a hole would be cut in the ice and a small shelter built over it to keep the fisherman in the dark. A lure would be dropped through the ice to attract the fish. Once the fish were close enough, they would be speared. At times, forty-foot spears were needed to reach the fish.

Young boys were also taught to make fish traps by placing rocks across a stream in the shape of a "V." The fish, once guided into the "V," were easily caught. When finished the trap would be dismantled, allowing other fish to move downstream to grow and reproduce.

Adult life for Native American children began between the ages of twelve and fourteen. One of the first steps in becoming an adult was to go on a vision quest. A vision quest experience is considered sacred and private. The practice faded over time, but, today, more and more Native Americans seek to experience such a quest.

The Odawa people believed that "No man begins to be until he has seen his vision" (Johnston) and that each man and woman had a personal gift or purpose in life. A vision quest would reveal that life's purpose. A purification ceremony was performed before sending a young man or woman to a remote location for fasting and isolation. During this time, a vision might or might not be realized. Vision quests would occur yearly until a vision was revealed. Females, in addition to having a life's purpose, also had the gift of giving life.

Wiigwaasabak, or birchbark scrolls, were the books of the tribe. Because the spoken language of the Odawa has only recently been put in written form, the information on the scrolls is in pictographs or drawings. The recorded teachings include songs, maps, shapes, and complex Odawa concepts collected over hundreds of years. Some birchbark scrolls can be found in museums, but most were hidden for their protection and have yet to be located.

Oral traditions were and remain powerful tools for the Odawa. Linguist Basil Johnston notes, "Stories provided guidance on hunger, courage, generosity, fidelity, creation, death, transformation, history, and all matters that related to life and being. On a simple level, a child could find meaning in them, but they could also be understood on deeper levels by adults and elders."

The core values running through all these systems of educational delivery were ingeniously simplistic:

1. Learn the tribe's ceremonial standards.
2. Respect your culture and tribe.
3. Respect your elders.

Although simply presented, the idea of culture is very complicated. For Native Americans, culture involved social responsibility, skill orientation, political participation, and spiritual and moral values. It included developing a healthy attitude toward honest labor, developing a sense of belonging, and encouraged active participation in community activities (Yeboah).

Throughout the century the Odawa spent on the Old Mission Peninsula, their methods of education and core values served them well. The tribes thrived. After contact with Europeans, the Odawa way of life was forever changed. Or perhaps it wasn't.

For hundreds of years, the United States government tried to beat the core values out of the Odawa and other Native American tribes. This history is tragic, but today the tribes are regaining strength in great part because their native languages are being taught, their history is being told by fellow Native Americans, and their ceremonial standards are once again being taught to old and young alike.

Site of the former Anishinaabek village in Old Mission. Today, this area is known as Kelley Park. Photo courtesy of Christopher Rieser.

References

A Tribal History of the Little Traverse Bay Bands of Odawa Indians. ltbbodawa-nsn.gov.

Eyaawing Museum and Cultural Center, Peshawbestown, Michigan. Pamphlet. 2017.

Fishing in the Western Great Lakes Region. Nativeamericanroots.net. May 15, 2012.

Johnston, Basil. *Ojibway Heritage.* University of Nebraska Press, Lincoln, 1990.

Kurt, Miighan. "Turtle Island: The Original Name for North America." mkimpexp@nativeweb.net http://ti.stats.sibirga.net.tripod.com/niiji.htm. Posted March 29, 2007.

"Mazina'igan, a Chronicle of the Lake Superior Ojibwe." *Telling Our Stories.* Spring 2018.

"Once upon a Time in Old Mission." *The Northern Michigan Journal.* Walter Johnson.

"Ottawa History." Tolatsoa.org.

Reese, Richard Adrian. "What Is Sustainable?" Powered by Blogger. July 16, 2012.

Reiser, Karen. "Three Sisters Plus One." Mynaturetales.com. June 5, 2016.

Toulouse, Isadore. Language and Cultural Instruction, Little Traverse Bay Band of Odawa Indians. Interview. Tuesday May 1, 2018.

www.farmlandinfo.org/sites/default/files/Peninsula_Township_Comprehensive_plan_1.pdf.

Yeboah, Alberta. "Education among Native Americans in the Periods before and after Contact with Europeans: An Overview." Paper presented at the annual National Association of Native American Studies Conference, Houston, Texas, February 14 to 19, 2005.

Chapter Three
Time of Contact

"Time of contact" refers to the time in history when Native Americans and Europeans became aware of one another. At the time Europeans were settling in North America, their culture believed in colonization. To colonize the New World, they believed, the Native Americans would need to be civilized, Christianized, and Europeanized (Yeboah). In the mid-nineteenth century, the United States government took on this task.

Various agreements or treaties were made between the U.S. government and the Native American communities. One such agreement was the Indian Removal Act of 1830. This treaty required Native Americans to move west of the Mississippi, leaving land open for white settlers.

Early settlers, hoping to improve their economic situations, were eager to move west. The ability of flatboats to move products up and down the Ohio River and the Erie Canal and an increase in the number of roads leading west made the move possible. Initially, the majority of settlers made their homes in the southern part of the Michigan territory, so the Native American settlement on the Old Mission Peninsula drew little attention.

In 1836, the Treaty of Washington was signed by some members of the Odawa tribe. In this treaty, the Native Americans ceded fourteen million acres of their lands to the United States for cash. These monies would pay off debt and provide food and supplies over the next twenty years. In return, the United States government promised to provide missions, schools, and reservations.

Not all the Odawa wanted to sign the 1836 Treaty of Washington. To prevent him from being influenced by the others, Chief Aghossa, along with several representatives from the tribe, were taken to Washington, D.C., away from the naysayers, to sign. After this trip, Chief Aghossa always wore a waistcoat and top hat.

Chief Aghossa, date unknown.
Photo taken from *100 Years from the Old Mission: A Century in Grand Traverse County 1839–1939* courtesy of Horizon Books.

The Treaty of Washington also cleared the way for the United States government to consider the Michigan territory for statehood. This act required a minimum population of sixty thousand residents. On January 26, 1837, with this number achieved, Michigan became the twenty-sixth state in the Union.

To fulfill the promise of a mission, school, and reservation, the U.S. government sent Henry Schoolcraft, an Indian agent, to make the arrangements. When seeking a site, his first choice was to build the mission and school in the present-day Bowers Harbor area. The deep harbor was perfect for the water travel of the day.

Schoolcraft, a faithful Presbyterian, contacted the Presbyterian Board of Foreign Missions (PBOFM) seeking its support in setting up the mission and school. After hiring a Native American named Mr. Greensky to serve as an interpreter, the PBOFM sent Reverend Peter Dougherty and Reverend John Fleming to take on the task. In May of 1839, traveling in their Mackinaw boat from Mackinac Island, the three men came ashore in what was then called "Grand Traverse Country" and is now referred to as Old Mission. A second boat filled with supplies was rowed ashore by four Native Americans.

Only one Native American was found occupying the small village the men had seen from the water. At that time, several Native American tribes were camped at the mouth of the Elk River in what is now Elk Rapids, and additional tribes were planning to move to the Elk River area. This can be considered the moment of contact, as Reverend Dougherty and Reverend Fleming were the first white people other than the French fur trappers who came and went to come to the area.

A chief and several Native Americans arrived the next day to investigate the situation. Several days later, the head chief, Chief Aish-qua-gwan-aba, came to speak to the Reverends Dougherty and Fleming. Reverend Dougherty told the chief that the two men had permission from the "Great White Father," the president of the United States, to start a mission and school in the area. Chief Aish-qua-gwan-aba agreed to the idea. The reverends left the Old Mission site and moved across the water to the Elk River site to set up their mission, but all did not go as expected. John Fleming, after receiving the news of his wife's death, departed, never to return, leaving Reverend Dougherty to create the mission on his own.

In addition to a school and mission, the Treaty of Washington required the federal government to provide a blacksmith, carpenter, educator, and farmer to advise and teach the Native Americans. Schoolcraft soon brought Isaac George, a blacksmith, to the peninsula, settling him at Mission Harbor. The carpenter, educator, and farmer followed, also settling at Mission Harbor.

Chief Aghossa and his tribe had been living at Mission Harbor but planned to move to the Elk River encampment. Peter Dougherty had been on the Elk River for a month when Chief Aghossa came to inform him that he and his tribe had decided to stay on the peninsula because they valued the deep waters of Mission Harbor. Chief Aghossa offered to build a house for the reverend (not the present-day Dougherty Mission House) and transport him across the bay if the reverend would build his mission on the peninsula at Mission Harbor instead of at the mouth of the Elk River.

Knowing that Chief Aghossa's tribe was the largest, Reverend Dougherty accepted the offer. Mr. Schoolcraft approved the Mission Harbor site, thus making it a reservation. The move was made, and school began the next day.

Mr. Greensky, the Native American interpreter, taught the first classes on Old Mission in a small bark wigwam. In 1840, the log house that had been built for the Elk Rapids mission was taken apart and brought to the Mission Harbor site. Once reconstructed, it served as a church, school, and woodshed. Two years later, Chief Aghossa and his tribe helped build a formal church along with the Peter Dougherty Mission House that today is preserved as a historical, educational, and cultural center in Old Mission. The structure brought over from the Elk River remained a school until it burned down in 1857.

Mr. Bradley was sent to replace Mr. Greensky as the educator. In the next twelve years, Mr. Bradley was replaced by Mr. Whiteside, who was replaced by Mr. Andrew Porter.

Both Native American and European children attended school. The white children were the children of the missionaries and settlers in the area. Peter Dougherty and his wife, Maria, had nine children, three of whom attended the school. Some Native American adults also attended school.

A formal Eurocentric system of education prevailed. Children sat on benches to receive instruction while teachers taught from charts displayed at the front of the class. As time went on, more formal educational materials became part of the school.

The goal of the education was to convert the Native Americans to Christianity and civilize them by teaching European culture. Students were taught to read, write, and speak English. Arithmetic, European culture, and religion were also taught. The Native Americans were forbidden to "speak Indian" or learn their native culture.

Once converted, the Native Americans wore European clothing, practiced Christianity, and received Christian names. Chief Aghossa was Reverend Dougherty's first convert. His name was changed from Aghossa to Addison Potts.

Life continued on the peninsula. The mission was filled with white-washed log homes rather than wigwams because Reverend Dougherty felt it gave the mission a civilized look. The Native Americans remained at the mission year-round, no longer seeking winter refuge to the south. Gardens, at some distance from the village, remained a mainstay of Native American life.

According to the Treaty of Washington, the Old Mission land was exclusively the Native Americans' to work for five years but did not belong to them. While the tribes were allowed to work the land long after the five-year limit was up, more and more white settlers were moving into the area who desired land. At the same time, the Indian Removal Act, approved in 1830, had promised to put Native Americans on reservations west of the Mississippi.

With these two factors in mind, the United States government began to talk about relocating the tribes. Chief Aghossa sent a group of people to investigate the land west of the Mississippi, but they returned with a very negative report. The tribe was unwilling to relocate to the west, although some members began to talk about moving to Canada.

Simultaneously, the State of Michigan's 1850 Constitution granted citizenship to Native Americans who had been converted, civilized, and were not members of a tribe. Chief Aghossa and many of his followers satisfied these requirements. As citizens, buying land from the United States government became possible.

The tribe earned money from selling animal hides, especially beaver. Reverend Dougherty accompanied the Native Americans to Mackinac Island to sell their furs. Once they were paid, a great many white traders offered to sell them "fire water," blankets, and trinkets. Instead, the Native Americans entrusted their money to Reverend Dougherty for safekeeping. This is how, when it became possible to purchase land, they had the funds to do it.

Nonetheless, they weren't allowed to buy land on the Old Mission Peninsula. This land had been a reservation for five years, and when the five years were up, no one was sure who it belonged to. Therefore, it wasn't for sale. Only after the Civil War did the federal government decide it owned the peninsula and begin to sell the land.

Reverend Dougherty advised the Native Americans of his mission to buy land across the bay on the Leelanau Peninsula. Some did so while others moved to Canada. Dougherty followed his flock across the bay and developed a new mission in 1852 in what is now known as Omena, which is said to mean, "It is so." This was one of Dougherty's favorite expressions.

Thereafter, the peninsula was casually referred to as "Old Mission" to differentiate it from the "New Mission." The title became official when postmaster George Hebben, appointed in February of 1869, changed the peninsula post office's name from the Grand Traverse Post Office to the Old Mission Peninsula Post Office.

It is interesting to note that the Native Americans who moved to Canada settled in a very remote location where the government took no interest in them. Consequently, their language, culture, and spirit were undiluted. The Grand Traverse Band of Ottawa and Chippewa Indians located in Omena has since invited many Native Americans from Canada to re-introduce the tribe's original culture, language, and spirit.

Restored Dougherty Mission House in 2019.
Photo courtesy of Christopher Rieser.

References

Native Americans: Missions and Schools–University of Michigan.
www.umich.edu/~bhlumrec/programs_centers/...edu/...native/missions.html.

Peninsula Township Master Plan, 2004, Grand Traverse County.
www.farmlandinfo.org/sites/default/files/Peninsula_Township_Comprehensive_plan_1.pdf.

Solomonson, Jack and Vi, and Lance, Mary Jo. *A Century of Service: The People and Places on Old Mission Peninsula.* Peninsula Telephone Company. 2008.

Yeboah, Alberta. "Education among Native Americans in the Periods before and after Contact with Europeans: An Overview." Paper presented at the annual National Association of Native American Studies Conference, Houston, Texas, February 14 to 19, 2005.

Chapter Four

All Aboard

One hundred seventy-four years ago, the *Madeline*, a Great Lakes schooner, carried freight back and forth across upper Lake Michigan. At that time, she was one of two thousand schooners sailing the Great Lakes.

Built in 1845 in Fairport, Ohio, this small two-masted vessel took on a very special role by becoming the first non-Indian school on the Old Mission Peninsula in the winter of 1851–'52.

At that time, a crew of five—William, Michael, and John Fitzgerald along with William Bryce and Edward Chambers, the cook—worked on the *Madeline*. The men were competent sailors but couldn't read, write, or do arithmetic. In their wisdom, they realized that, to be truly successful, they needed to acquire these skills. Since there could be no winter sailing on the ice-covered lakes, they decided to hire a teacher and spend the winter in a quiet harbor.

In the fall of 1851, the men chose Bowers Harbor as the site for their educational adventure. The harbor was deep with few distractions, and there they turned the *Madeline's* cabin into a classroom, hiring seventeen-year-old S. E. Wait to teach them reading, writing, and arithmetic, "the three Rs," for $20.00 in gold a month.

Throughout the winter of 1851–'52, mornings were spent in the classroom. Afternoons were reserved for chores, wood cutting, and snowball fights. When spring arrived, the crew emerged as readers, writers, and mathematicians, and each and every one of them went off to have a successful career sailing the Great Lakes.

One of the Fitzgerald grandsons, a man named Edmund, eventually owned and operated the insurance company by the same name. His name was chosen to adorn the tanker *Edmund Fitzgerald*.

As for S. E. Wait, he became a well-known photographer, builder, and sailor and owned the town pharmacy. Today, a plaque secured to a rock can be found on the beach of Bowers Harbor not far from the Boathouse restaurant honoring Mr. Wait.

Modern replica of the schooner *Madeline*.
Photo courtesy of Christopher Rieser.

References

"*Madeline*, the Original *Madeline*." maritimeheritagealliance.org.

Meyers, Julianne E. "One-Room Schools, Reflections of Yesterday." 1988.

Peninsula Township Master Plan. Grand Traverse County, Michigan. 2004. *Old Mission Peninsula History, Demographics, and Geography*. Early Peninsula History. farmlandinfor.org.

Chapter Five

School Is Where the Students Are

Sometime in the 1850s, Joseph and Mary Hesler (sometimes spelled "Hessler") sailed west on the Saint Lawrence River to Mackinac Island before continuing on to the Old Mission Peninsula. They chose to settle on the southern end of the peninsula facing East Bay across from the present-day Underwood Farms development. Like most pioneers, Joseph and Mary were immigrants, Joseph having come from Canada and Mary from Ireland.

Once on the peninsula, Joseph and Mary dreamed of creating a farm. With the help of their neighbors, one a carpenter, another a shingle maker, and another a cooper, they erected an 18- x 20-foot log house. Using the timber found in the area, they placed dovetailed hand-hewn logs chinked with plaster on a stone foundation.

On June 7, 1859, the Heslers moved into their modest home. There, with a great deal of effort, they raised wheat, corn, potatoes, and fruit trees. A sugarbush located at the back of the property provided maple syrup.

After a little more than a decade, the Heslers sold their 133.48-acre farm to Benjamin Travis. Mr. Travis logged the land for two years before selling it to John A. Coughran. The log home was abandoned for some time.

A neighbor's daughter, Clementina Holdsworth, came to the area when she was eight years old. There was no school in the area, so school was held in her home. The following year, when the McMullen's son became old enough to attend, school was held in the McMullen's new barn. The following year, the abandoned log house on Center Road, the Hesler log cabin, was used as the school.

Next, Francis Hughes, a Chicago businessman, bought the property. During the 1920s and '30s, he established a large dairy farm on the land on which the log cabin stood. He chose to house a bull in the cabin, his bachelor quarters. In the 1950s, prior to mechanical cherry harvesters, migrant workers used the cabin as their shelter. Finally, in 1992, a developer bought the property and planned to demolish the cabin.

This was not acceptable to the Old Mission Peninsula community, which by now had swelled to 4,600 people, and a group of concerned citizens formed. Members included individuals from the Peninsula Township Board of Trustees, the Peninsula Township Park Board, the Old Mission Peninsula Historical Society, the Old Mission Women's Club, the Old Mission Elementary School, the American Legion, and the Garden Club. Money was successfully raised to relocate, protect, and restore the Heslers' early home.

In 1992, the cabin was moved to Lighthouse Park at the tip of the peninsula. Mr. Walter Johnson, a local farmer, donated lumber and logs to be used for restoration. Many volunteers worked to restore this piece of the peninsula's history, and today the Old Mission Peninsula Historical Society maintains the cabin.

Still a school, the Hesler Log Cabin teaches young and old alike about pioneer living on the peninsula. Peek in its windows, visit the viewing area, and study the furnishings for an eye-opening experience. Annually, Michigan third graders visit the site to enhance their understanding of Michigan history.

If school is where the students are, the Hesler Log Cabin will forever be a teacher.

Hesler Log Cabin located in Lighthouse Park at the tip of the Old Mission Peninsula. Photo courtesy of Christopher Rieser.

References

1. Echos Newsletter, Old Mission Peninsula Historical Society, Vol.1 No. 1, The Hessler Log House, Flo Schermerhorn, Spring 2004.

2. Solomonson, Jack and Vi, and Lance, Mary Jo. *A Century of Service: The People and Places on Old Mission Peninsula.* Peninsula Telephone Company. 2008

Chapter Six

The Era of the One-Room Schoolhouse

Moving the mission across the bay in 1852 did not diminish the need for education on the Old Mission Peninsula, which continued to see an influx of settlement.

The log school that had served the mission continued to serve the settlers until 1857 when it was destroyed by fire. A new school, the Old Mission School, was built within the year in the village of Old Mission.

The new Old Mission School consisted of a grammar room, library, and hall and initially enrolled twenty-five students. A primary room, two cloakrooms, a basement, two furnaces, and an entrance were added in 1889. The school was the pride of the village.

As the population on the peninsula swelled, more schools were needed. In total, there came to be seven districts and seven one-room schoolhouses.

Each school was reportedly built so that no child would have to walk more than a mile to a mile and a half to school, but this assertion is vehemently disputed by many former students. Not only was the walk longer than a mile, but it was uphill both ways!

Old Mission School, circa 1857, was located at 18328 Old Mission Road. Photo courtesy of Christopher Rieser.

Stoney Beach School, circa 1859, was located at 9160 Montague. Photo courtesy of Christopher Rieser.

McKinley School, circa 1862, named for President William McKinley, was located at the corner of Center and McKinley roads. Photo courtesy of Christopher Rieser.

Bowers Harbor School, circa 1864, was located at the corner of Neahtawanta and Kroupa roads. Photo courtesy of Christopher Rieser.

Mapleton School, circa 1865, was located on the corner of Devils Dive and Seven Hills roads. The school burned down in 1973 when it was a private residence. A new home was later built on the old school's foundation. The school's flagpole can still be seen in the yard. Photo courtesy of Jack and Vi Solomonson and Mary Jo Lance, *A Century of Service*.

The Archie School, located in the vicinity of today's Archie Park on Center Road, was built on land donated by A. P. Gray around 1883. Sadly, the log school burned down in 1893. There are no known surviving photos.

Ogdensburg School,
circa 1884, was located
at 16213 Center Road.
Photo courtesy
of Christopher Rieser.

Maple Grove School,
circa 1904, was located
at 11480 Center Road.
Photo courtesy
of Christopher Rieser.

One-Room Schoolhouse Timeline

1857–1955	Old Mission School
1859–1955	Stoney Beach School
1862–1955	McKinley School
1864–1955	Bowers Harbor School
1865–1955	Mapleton School
Around 1883–1893	Archie School
1884–1955	Ogdensburg School
1896–1958	Maple Grove School

The phrase "one-room schoolhouse" typically brings to mind a building with one room, hence the name. Though this was often the case, most one-room schoolhouses had multiple rooms. The phrase might have emanated from the system of educational delivery since K–8 students were placed in one room to receive their education.

A typical day in a one-room schoolhouse began with the ringing of the bell. Many schools had an entrance for girls and a separate entrance for boys. Teachers were greeted with the best of manners, perhaps a bow or curtsey. The boys sat on one side of the room while the girls occupied the other side. The number of students varied from six to forty or more. The youngest sat in front, the oldest in the back, with the teacher's desk located at the front of the room on a platform. Eventually, shelves and benches were replaced by desks that were often nailed to the floor. The woodburning stove used to heat the room was later replaced by a furnace. Outhouses served as bathrooms until indoor plumbing made it onto the scene.

As it is today, the playground was a magic place. The boys had their side and the girls had the other, with an imaginary dividing line no one dared cross. Boys made up games and played marbles, ball, and sometimes tusseled. Not lacking imagination, girls also made up games and enjoyed jump rope, jacks, and playing house.

Teachers were literate in all the subjects they taught but had no formal training in educational practices. Reading, writing, and arithmetic were the core subjects, but history and geography were also studied. The lessons students were assigned matched their abilities, not their ages or grades.

At the time of the one-room schoolhouse, paper and educational materials were scarce. This scarcity defined educational practices, which relied upon memorizing and reciting a vast quantity of information. All addition, subtraction, division, and multiplication facts had to be memorized, and word problems had to be solved mentally.

The first reader children learned from was the Bible. Later came the McGuffy Readers. From primer to level five, the McGuffy Readers taught reading, morals, and values such as honesty, courage, charity, and good manners. Schools that were able to meet the standards of the state board of education, including the original Old Mission School, were called standard schools.

According to peninsula resident Lois Lardie Steffes, at the turn of the century, the Old Mission School supported so many students that another class had to be added. Unfortunately, there was no space for this class, so an addition was needed. Philip Devol allowed the children to use the upstairs of his house for their schooling until the addition was completed.

After nearly ten years of use, in 1893, the little Archie School made of logs burned to the ground. To replace it, two new school districts were created, and the McKinley and Stoney Beach Schools were erected.

Mr. Frank French donated the land on the corner of Montague and Center roads for the McKinley School building named for President McKinley.

The Stoney Beach School had two entrances, one for the boys and one for the girls. As a result of increased enrollment in 1908, an addition that housed the lower grades was added. By 1915, enrollment had dropped and only one room was used.

Maple Grove School was built in 1896. Township records from 1920 show the female teacher was paid $100.00 a month. From that salary, she paid $5.00 to the janitor and $12.50 for her room and board. As was customary, male teachers received a 50% higher salary than female teachers.

I sat down with several former students who attended the one-room schools on the Old Mission Peninsula. One student informed me that, "Taking my lunch to school on homemade bread was frustrating; one side was always larger than the other." Another student commented, "We didn't have plastic wrap in those days, and the newspaper my mom wrapped my sandwiches in always left black smudges on my bread." During World War II, a third student recalled that, students at Old Mission School were given a day off to collect milkweed seed pods to be used as a filler for floatation devices for servicemen.

All the peninsula children attended high school in Traverse City. There, the Traverse City students looked down on them as "farmers" from the peninsula. Because they were bussed in, most of the Old Mission students had to leave right after school. There was no time for extracurricular activities. If they'd stayed, they would have needed to find a ride home, which for most would have meant hitchhiking.

Without question, the era, the social conditions, and the location of each school played a pivotal role in the education the three former students highlighted below received.

Jerry L. Ostlund,
June 27, 2018.
Photo courtesy
of Christopher Rieser.

The Ostlund family arrived on the Old Mission Peninsula during the 1800s. Their original homestead was the white house across from the general store in Old Mission. This house welcomed Jerry's father into the world and Jerry and his mother home from the hospital.

Their home had no running water. The kitchen contained an old-fashioned stove and an icebox that required a block of ice and a drip pan. A daily chore for Jerry's father was bringing water to the house that he poured into a reservoir in the stove. The back shed held a chemical toilet and a shower made from a hose stuck inside a bucket full of holes. Jerry remembers showers being mighty short! Later, his father bought the house down the street where Jerry lives today. The family then had the modern conveniences of indoor plumbing and kitchen appliances plus forty acres of cherries to tend. In addition to working his farm, Jerry's father worked as a sharecropper for the Rushmore family.

Jerry's mother was a teacher at the Old Mission School. She had attended Central Michigan University in Mount Pleasant, Michigan, where she earned her teaching certificate. Each summer, Jerry recalled, she took classes to improve her teaching.

Jerry began in the primary room in Old Mission School in the village of Old Mission in 1940. His day began at 8:00 a.m. and ended at 3:30 p.m. In those days everyone walked to school regardless of the weather. There were no snow days, though there was an occasional ice day or two.

Students entered Old Mission School through a set of big iron doors. After opening the doors, they found themselves in the entryway where the bell cord hung. A short distance down the hall to the right was a cloakroom complete with old black iron hooks in a straight line. A door from the cloakroom led to the "little room" and the "big room."

The little room was the primary room where Jerry's mother taught. Jerry's mother was also his first teacher, which he describes as, "Not too swift." The big room housed the first through eighth grades with Verna Musser as the teacher. In the center between the two rooms were the bathrooms.

The basement held a full kitchen and picnic tables. Local residents did the cooking, one of whom was Jerry's Aunt Olive. Some of the cooking, such as soups and stews, was done at home and brought to the school on sleds. The government provided turkeys and tremendous amounts of butter, cheese, and canned goods. Two of the older students were sent downstairs each day to help the cook. They set the tables using real silverware and dishes, stayed to help during lunch, wiped down the tables after lunch, and helped clean the kitchen.

Old Mission School was heated with a coal furnace. Charlie Crampton, the school's janitor, lived on Traverse Road. He would arrive early to stoke the furnace, stoke it again at noon, and bank it at night for the next day. Jerry recalls that the school was always warm.

The children of local farmers and Native American field workers attended Old Mission School. There were between twelve and fifteen children in each room. The primary room was large with no teacher platform. It had a wall of windows that opened on the west side of the room. There was a platform raising the teacher's desk above the students and a wall of windows on the south side of the big room.

At Old Mission School, older students didn't teach younger children. Lessons were taught by the teacher. Paper, pencils, and the black slate board were the main teaching tools, and reading, writing, and arithmetic were taught every day. Addition, subtraction, multiplication, and division were taught using the slate boards, and reading was taught with the Dick and Jane readers. Geography was also taught, though not every day. There was no gym or art, but there was music. A teacher named Mr. Weston taught Jerry to play a plastic recorder.

Like most children, Jerry loved recess. There was a morning recess and recess after lunch. Red Rover, sledding, and jump rope were popular games. It was hard to jump rope on the dirt playground, Jerry recalled, so the kids often went to Lardie's store to jump on the concrete. The store was also a favorite spot after school to buy penny candy and junk food.

Sledding at school was particularly fun. The students kept their sleds at school all week and took them home on the weekends. At Old Mission School, they would slide down the slope on the northwest side, around the school, and down the road. At Mapleton School, Seven Hills Road was a great sliding area.

As for discipline, the mere mention of the word brought a smile to Jerry's face. In school, he admitted, he was always laughing. Something would occur, and he would laugh. Having been caught laughing, he was always assumed to be the culprit.

One day, Jerry recalled, for some forgotten deed, Mrs. Musser had him bend over a chair to be spanked with a paddle filled with holes. Did that ever hurt! Another punishment was cleaning erasers.

Later, when Jerry rode to Traverse City on the school bus, he met Shorty, his bus driver. Whenever there was a problem on the bus, Shorty would look in his mirror and see Jerry laughing. Then, when the bus stopped at Jerry's house, Shorty would make him sweep the entire bus with a tiny broom before letting him off. Of course, his father would see this and know that Jerry was in trouble even before he got into the house.

Two major events occurred each year at schools on the Old Mission Peninsula. The first was the Christmas program, and the second was softball season.

The Christmas program was the pride of the community. Teachers created the programs, the primary students acted out the nativity scenes and sang, and the children from the big room performed a play written by the teacher. At Old Mission School, the play had to be memorized, but students at Mapleton School had scripts.

Starting before Thanksgiving, students would march from school to the former Old Mission Legion Hall where there was a raised stage with curtains and a large seating area for practice. Sometime around December 20, the entire community would gather at the legion to enjoy the antics of their children.

Then there was softball. Each school had a softball team and a well-developed sense of competition. Friday afternoons, the teams would travel to each other's schools. The entire community loved to watch and root for their school.

When his mother left her position as the primary teacher at Old Mission to teach in the Mapleton School, Jerry moved with her. He completed the fifth, sixth, and seventh grades at Mapleton, but there was only one other student in the eighth grade. Seeking a sense of community for their son, Jerry's parents scratched together the tuition and sent him to Traverse City for his eighth-grade year.

Looking back, one of Jerry's most striking recollections concerned the strong bonds that developed between the students at Old Mission School. The relationship between a group of ten children who lived within walking distance of one another, played together, worked the fields together, summered at Haserot Beach together, gathered for parties at Lighthouse Park, and went through school together is still evident today.

All but a few of these children left Old Mission to embark on their careers. Jerry ended up in Chicago and Saint Louis working for the Chicago Northwestern Railroad. After forty-two years, he returned to his family homestead. Retirement has brought the others back as well.

In addition to monthly meetings, they gather for lunch every Sunday after church at the Old Mission Tavern.

That's the real benefit of learning in a one-room schoolhouse, even if it did have two rooms.

Timothy Carroll, August 17, 2018.
Photo courtesy
of Christopher Rieser.

The Carrolls were members of the first wave of European settlers to arrive on the Old Mission Peninsula. Patrick Carroll, Tim's great-great-grandfather, arrived in America with his parents from County Louth, Ireland. All eight of Tim's great-grandparents were in Traverse City by the 1850s. One set of great-grandparents, Richard and Mary Rice Johnson, met in Traverse City in the early 1850s. Theirs was the eighth marriage recorded in the courthouse. Shortly after their marriage, they moved to the Mapleton School District on the peninsula and built the house Tim lives in today.

Tim's grandmother, Daisy Isabel, was born in the family home in 1881. She met and married Alex Carroll, one of seven brothers and three sisters in the Edward Carroll family, who lived on what is today Carroll Road in the former Maple Grove School District.

Daisy and Alex raised six children. Tim's father, Fred, the only son, took on the responsibilities of the cherry farm and built a house next door for his bride, Norma Wilhelm. Tim, his brother, and sister all had the good fortune to grow up next door to the best chocolate chip cookie maker on the peninsula, his grandmother Daisy.

Tim loved to learn, and the family loved to travel. Each Christmas, when his father received his AAA atlas from the insurance company, Tim would pore over every map. The family visited Tucson, New Orleans, Miami, New Mexico, and Canada, stopping at every roadside museum and attraction they found. The Carroll family had a passion to see the world, a passion Tim displayed throughout his career and in his retirement.

In 1944, at age five, Tim began his formal education. School seemed like an extension of home, and he loved it. He attended Mapleton School, located at the corner of Devils Dive and Seven Hills Road, from kindergarten through seventh grade. From there, he went to Saint Francis in Traverse City and then on to Notre Dame.

The Mapleton School consisted of a large room divided by great sliding doors. The rooms were the same size but were referred to as the "big" and the "little" rooms; Tim recalled that these names were given to match the size of the children occupying them. At times, both rooms were full. At other times, such as during WWII, there weren't enough children to fill two rooms. In addition to the classrooms, there was a cloakroom and eventually a lunchroom.

A class size of six children was typically the rule. Classes included the children of farmers and hired men. There was no drama between the children regardless of age. Bullying didn't exist even between the boys and girls, Tim recalled, because the girls were just as tough as the boys.

The first day of school meant heading into Traverse City to buy schoolbooks. Arnold's on West Front Street was the place to go with its wooden floors, old store smell, crowds, and huge social studies and history books. Of course, Tim's favorite purchase was a box of brand-new Crayola crayons.

Mrs. Brush was Tim's kindergarten, first, and second grade teacher. For fourth through the sixth grades, Mrs. Valley was his instructor. As a child, Tim was sure that all teachers must be named after nature until Mrs. Musser arrived to teach the seventh grade. It was Mrs. Valley who skipped Tim from the third grade to the fourth grade, as he was the only student in third grade that year. Despite this leap of convenience, Tim did well.

Each day, Tim would jump out of bed, get dressed, eat a hasty breakfast, and run through the orchard to school, which was located at the corner of his family's farm. School began at 8:00 a.m., and if you were in the upper grades, you were allowed to ring the bell using the rope hanging in the cloakroom or raise the flag. Raising the flag meant you must know how to fold it.

School work began as soon as the children entered the classroom. Students sat at their desks to do their seatwork while others were called forward for their recitations. The teacher sat at the front of the room with three large two-seated chairs in front of her. The students would come forward, recite their lessons, and receive instruction. As the children did their seatwork, they heard what all the other grades were learning. This provided a constant review for those who needed more time to acquire the necessary skills to move on.

Older children, fourth through sixth graders, taught the kindergarteners their ABCs and numbers in the cloakroom. Tim clearly remembers learning in the cloakroom but does not remember his cousin's story of working with him as he tried to "kiss on her."

After a mid-morning recess of fifteen minutes, it was back to work. Next it was lunch time. Everyone opened their lunch pails except Tim, who ran home for lunch. As a kindergartener, it was unnecessary for him to return, but he always did.

After lunch recess, the afternoon began with read-aloud time. *Anne of Green Gables* and *Heidi* were some of Tim's favorite books. Studies continued throughout the afternoon. First graders were allowed to go home at two o'clock, but Tim always stayed.

Lessons were integrated across all subjects, so it was hard to tell where one subject left off and another began. As a fifth grader, when your work was complete, you were to occupy yourself with other learning activities. Tim's favorite activity was to pull down an enormous globe suspended from the ceiling by pulleys. He studied the globe as much as he could. His greatest pleasure came the day he found the Old Mission Peninsula. Tim's future held a tremendous amount of world travel, but this early lesson assured him that he could always find his way home.

At the end of the day, there was no homework. Who could carry all those books across the fields and orchards? Besides, there were evening chores to do.

Once a month, Mrs. Cornell, the county health nurse, visited the school. She was a bird-like lady in a well-starched uniform and clodhopper shoes who smelled of astringent. She inspected all their fingernails and explained the horrors of getting worms. Tim never forgot her lesson on bad habits.

As she wrote the word "Habits" on the board, she announced that bad habits were the worst habits to have because they were very hard to get rid of. She then proceeded to erase the "H," saying, "See, you still have 'abit' left." Erasing the "A," she said, "There are still 'bits' left." Finally, the "B" was erased, but "it" was still left. Thanks to this lesson, Tim realized that he did need to beware of bad habits because they were very hard to get rid of.

In seventh grade, the basement was made into a lunchroom. Mrs. Lindsey was the cook and made hot meals for everyone. Her special treat was making a birthday cake for every child on their special day. Alas, Tim was not always pleased with the lunch menu. One day, he decided he could not swallow Mrs. Lindsey's potato soup and told her so. He had to do without lunch that day, but the next time potato soup was served, it was somehow a bit easier to swallow.

Unlike Jerry Ostlund, Tim did not need the paddle, though he did receive a reprimand or two. By seventh grade, he felt very much in charge of the classroom. When the new teacher, Mrs. Musser, introduced herself, he raised his hand and asked if she preferred to be called "Mrs. Musser" or "teacher." Mrs. Musser replied, "Do you prefer to be called 'Tim' or 'boy'?" Tim held his tongue the rest of the year.

Teacher's Institute gave the students a two-day break from school each fall. One year, Tim remembers his teacher coming back with a flat metal box the size of a piece of paper. Under its lid was some sort of gelatin. With a purple pencil, the teacher could write something on it, lay paper over it, and rub. Seven copies of the same paper could be made using this device. Now they each could have a copy of a test paper! When left overnight, the writing sank into the jelly.

The highlight of the school year for all the one-room schoolhouses was the Christmas pageant. The doors between the rooms were opened. The parents brought in sawhorses and built a stage. There were musty green curtains, curtain pullers, and even an offstage. Soon, rehearsal began. Day after day, the students practiced.

Tim clearly remembers playing a character named Rasmus. Rasmus was pushing Petunia, a pleasingly plump girl, to the county fair in a wheelbarrow. Rasmus' opening line was, "Petunia, you are my better half." Petunia then responded, "Honey, I am your better seven-eighths!" to the roar of the audience.

If you could play an instrument, you were also part of the Christmas pageant's music presentation. It was a Carroll family rule that each child play an instrument, and Tim chose the clarinet. He had taken a few lessons at Minema Music Store and was mediocre at best when he volunteered to fill an empty spot in the annual pageant. Beforehand, Tim's father questioned his son's decision to play with so few lessons, but Tim decided to do his best. On the way home from the pageant, Tim's father apologized for doubting his son and pronounced Tim's playing a job well done.

The classroom was Tim's happy place, but school grounds were different. His athletic ability was limited. He was never able to catch a ball, and throwing it was equally difficult. He did what he could and tried to enjoy himself, but in his last years, the schools developed a softball league. This was a disaster for Tim. No matter what, he had to play so that the team would have nine players. No one, including Tim, was thrilled about this.

Throughout the school year, Friday nights were set aside for square dancing. All the teens from the seven different schools would meet at the township hall and dance until ten in the evening. Bob Sanborn was the faithful caller, teaching the boys and girls the joys of square dancing. Relationships formed during these dances that developed into dates, marriages, children, and grandchildren. The dances weren't held during the summer because the students were needed to help with the harvest.

Tim's time at Mapleton School passed quickly. After high school and college, he began a career with the United States government representing the U.S. in various positions in embassies in Pakistan, Poland, and Russia. Working as the protocol officer for Attorney General Janet Reno was the highlight of his career. If you ask Tim to describe his life's work, he will tell you, "I rejoiced in its variety."

After many years, Tim found his way back to the Old Mission Peninsula, as his love for the area never waned. The early lesson of realizing he would always be able to find his way home is as alive and well today as it was when he was a child. In his retirement, Tim continues to fill his life with exotic travel and adventure.

Cal Jamison, February 4, 2019. Photo courtesy of Christopher Rieser.

The Jameson family has been an important farming family on the Old Mission Peninsula for generations. Cal Jameson, having retired from farming, spent the majority of his life living and working in the footsteps of his forefathers.

As a small boy, in 1938, Cal enrolled in the Mapleton School. He actually lived on the line separating the Mapleton and Ogdensburg districts and could have enrolled in either school, but after some consideration, his father realized Cal's journey to the Ogdensburg School would be very hilly, so he enrolled Cal in the Mapleton School. There, Cal found the majority of his classmates were Catholic. The Jamesons were not Catholic, so on the days St. Michael's church taught catechism, Cal found himself in the classroom alone.

Mr. Fred Garland drove a Sinclair Oil truck to deliver oil to the farmers on the peninsula. Oil was used for farm work while wood was used to heat the homes. On his own, with no announcement, Mr. Garland arranged his route so that he would pass Cal in the morning and give him a ride to school.

Cal liked school for its social benefits. He knew academics were necessary for success in life, but as far as he was concerned, the goal of the one-room schoolhouse was to teach him to read and write well enough to attend middle school in Traverse City.

Shaking his head, smiling a crooked smile, Cal recalled a young schoolteacher from Detroit who came to the peninsula with her daughter to enjoy the blessings of rural life. Evidently, in Detroit, she had taught with a principal who had taken care of all the discipline, leaving her lacking in such skills. On the peninsula, she faced a challenging group of boys who tortured her with their behavior. She did not discipline them, nor did she share their antics with their parents.

One of the boys' favorite activities, Cal remembered, was tipping the bell. If you hung onto the bell rope long enough, the bell would tip and be unable to ring. To right the bell required a trip up into the belfry. Of course, this stopped class. It also gave the boys an opportunity to peek up the teacher's skirts.

On Devils Dive, where the recycling center is located, there was a pond that popped with bluegill. Cal recalled how recess seemed like a good time to fish and then return to school, or maybe not.

Another favorite activity, Cal admitted, was disabling the teacher's Model A. The boys, familiar with engines from tractors to cars, would shut off the gas valve to the carburetor, starving the car of gas. When the teacher tried to leave, she was out of luck. The boys would fix the car the next day.

The teacher lasted four months, then off she and her daughter went for a kinder, gentler experience. Today, in all his wisdom, Cal cannot understand why he and his friends behaved as they did. Shaking his head, he admitted, "We were horrible brats."

Next to arrive was Mrs. Huggar. She lived on the Old Mission Peninsula but had spent time teaching in Alaska. Cal and his buddies were very impressed with her ability to swing her yardstick across the room without ever missing her target. They were equally impressed with her ability to communicate with their parents. Discipline was now alive and well at the Mapleton School, but this didn't stop adventure outside the classroom.

A favorite winter recess activity was sneaking water out of the restroom and pouring it down Seven Hills Road. When the road iced up, you could have a wild ride for approximately a mile and a half to the bottom of the road.

On one of these sliding days, Cal and his buddies, feeling very manly, decided to help a family chopping wood at the side of the road. A friend asked to borrow Cal's sled. When he handed it back to Cal, he accidentally jammed Cal's fingers between the sawhorse and the sled's runners, cutting off the tips of Cal's middle and ring fingers.

The boys quickly headed back to school, where they wrapped Cal's fingers with a rubber band and twisted them with a pencil to make a tourniquet. It took a while to find a car in the neighborhood that ran, but once they did, Cal was off to Munson. After a week in the hospital, his fingers, albeit a bit shorter, healed. No big deal, and in the hospital, Cal discovered his love for oranges and orange candy slices.

Adventure continued outside the one-room schoolhouse. One day, Cal and his friend Terry decided they would build a fort across the road from the schoolhouse. They chose to chop down small diameter ash trees to make their fort. Now they needed horses to drag the trees to the building sight. They chose four of their friends to play horse. The four "horses" dragged the wood to the site, and there it stayed, never to become a fort.

The most important recess activity was softball. Mrs. Lindsey, the cook, served fabulous meals at lunchtime, but the boys gobbled their food in order to be dismissed to recess. After all, the first one dismissed got to be pitcher, the second one batter, and so on. Cal's mother said he lost all his table manners each year when softball season began.

Practice, practice, practice. Spring and summer games between schools were a community event. His eyes sparkling, Cal recalled one name that still stands out when he thinks back on softball season: Miss Antoinette, a.k.a. Tony, McManus, Senator George McManus's daughter. She was the pitcher for Maple Grove School, and when she pitched, no one hit.

Cal's father died when he was fourteen. Cal took an active role in caring for the farm that continued even after his mother remarried, but he never missed a day of school to work the farm.

After Mapleton School, Cal moved on to the middle school in Traverse City. High school was next, and there he discovered football. To play, you had to have good grades, so he studied hard and played hard. Once he graduated from high school, Cal enrolled at Michigan State University, where he took business, animal husbandry, and horticultural classes that helped him become a successful farmer. Today, he continues to consult and teach others in the community.

Without question, the comradery of the one-room schoolhouse was lost in later years once students left the peninsula to be educated elsewhere. Also, without question, students who attended the seven one-room schoolhouses on the Old Mission Peninsula are glad they did.

1910 Bowers Harbor School
Ila Tannewitz, teacher. Back row: Ruth Stanek, Rose Stanek, Clara Kroupa are all that were identified.

The teacher and students of Bowers Harbor School in 1910.
Photo courtesy of Jack and Vi Solomonson and Mary Jo Lance, *A Century of Service*.

References

Carroll, Tim. Interview. August 17, 2018.

Jamison, Cal. Interview. February 4, 2019.

Meyers, Julianne E. "One-Room Schools, Reflections of Yesterday." *Schools.* 1988.

Michigan One Room Schoolhouses: Grand Traverse County. michiganoneroomschoolhouses.blogspot.com.

One-Room Schoolhouse. American Library. www.americanslibrary.gov/es_ny_school_1.htmi.

One-Room Schoolhouse. Buchanan County, Iowa Historical Society. www.buchanancountyhistory.com.

Ostlund, Jerry. Interview. June 27, 2018

Solomonson, Jack and Vi, and Lance, Mary Jo. *A Century of Service: The People and Places on Old Mission Peninsula.* Peninsula Telephone Co. 2008.

www.farmlandinfo.org/sites/default/files/Peninsula_Township_Comprehensive_plan_1.pdf.

Chapter Seven

Consolidation

With time, all things change. Increased enrollment, concern over a consistent curriculum, and the school bus were just three reasons people began rethinking the benefits of the one-room schoolhouse.

As was the case in rural communities elsewhere, the idea of consolidating all seven schools began floating around the Old Mission Peninsula in the early 1950s. As consolidation became more and more likely, residents began weighing in.

Many individuals wanted the separate school districts maintained. The schools defined their communities both socially and culturally. They believed that smaller schools provided more individual instruction and continuous review as older students taught younger students. Many felt that moving away from the neighborhood school would mean their children spent far too much time on a bus.

Other people felt that consolidation would provide a consistent curriculum, be more financially advantageous, and provide for extras such as foreign language, special education, libraries, and specialized teachers and administrators.

Meetings were held, discussions ensued, and concerns and opinions were shared. In 1955, the idea was put to a vote: consolidation it was.

A plot of land on Island View Road was donated by Tom and Irene Hoffman for the new structure. In 1955, township residents authorized a bond to fund the school, and construction began. Local residents-built playgrounds and held fundraisers to purchase playground equipment.

It took a little more than a year to complete the new school. During this time, a plan to make the transition for students, educators, and the community as smooth as possible was implemented. Each one-room schoolhouse became home to students of one grade from all over the peninsula. The Old Mission School, having two separate rooms, assigned one room to the fifth grade and the other to the sixth. This gave all the students the opportunity to get to know one another and begin learning together.

Old Mission Peninsula School opened in 1956 with 305 students in kindergarten through the eighth grade. After eighth grade, students were bussed to the high schools in either Elk Rapids or Traverse City.

Construction of Old Mission Peninsula
School in 1954–'55. Photos courtesy of the
Peninsula Community Library Historical
Collection.

Providing the "extras," one of which was a school library, proved financially difficult for the new school, but the residents of Old Mission had always valued a community library. After all, they'd voted to establish one way back in 1859. For fifty-one years, that library was located in the private residence of Eugene Umlor, just north of Mapleton. In 1910 the community decided to divide the library between the seven one-room schoolhouses.

With consolidation, the question of the community library's location needed to be reconsidered. It was suggested that the township place the library in the new school. This was a novel idea: a public library within a public school! After a great deal of promotion and work by a great many volunteers, the idea was approved.

Peninsula Community Library, housing all the books from the one-room schoolhouses, opened on a warm summer day in 1957. Initially, the books were placed on the stage in the back of the gym. In 2005 and 2006, when the school was renovated, the library and its services were also enhanced.

References

"Education in Rural America during the 1950s and 60s." https://livinghistoryfarm.org/farmingin the50s/life_12.html.

Rieser, Karen. "Notable Women of the Old Mission Peninsula: A Sampler." *The Library Ladies.* 2014.

Solomonson, Jack and Vi, and Lance, Mary Jo. *A Century of Service: The People and Places on Old Mission Peninsula.* Peninsula Telephone Company. 2008

Chapter Eight

The State of Michigan Upsets the Balance

A bit more than a year after consolidation, on October 4, 1957, the Russians launched *Sputnik 1*. The size of a beachball, the world's first artificial satellite orbited the Earth every ninety-eight minutes for three months.

Americans felt shocked and demoralized and began questioning their own abilities as a super technological power. Many feared that *Sputnik 1* highlighted a national problem with education.

Congress agreed. In 1958, it passed the National Defense Education Act to enhance education in the areas of math and science, and the race to space was on. Since then, educational competition between countries and educational legislation has been prolific on both the state and federal levels.

The State of Michigan had the next great impact on education on the Old Mission Peninsula. In 1964, Public Act 289 began requiring all school districts in Michigan to provide a K–12 education. The Old Mission School District consisting of Old Mission Peninsula School provided for grades K–8. Consequently, in 1968, Old Mission Peninsula School became Old Mission Elementary School and part of the newly formed district called Traverse City Area Public Schools (TCAPS). All its busses and property were transferred to TCAPS.

Over time, the Old Mission Elementary School came to serve grades K–5, with grades 6,7, and 8 bussed to the Traverse City middle schools.

Old Mission Elementary School evolved into a magical place of learning and growing for grades K–5. Sitting on a bluff overlooking the west arm of Grand Traverse Bay amid cherry orchards, the school sported a spring-fed pond, a woods filled with maple trees, and a sugar shack. Within the classrooms, dedicated teachers, support staff, diligent administrators, and hard-working parents provided a superior education.

For forty-seven years, academic life was good. Then, everything changed.

References

Solomonson, Jack and Vi, and Lance, Mary Jo. *A Century of Service: The People and Places on Old Mission Peninsula.* Peninsula Telephone Company. 2008.

"Sputnik and the Dawn of the Space Age." History.nasa.gov

Chapter Nine

An Unexpected 180

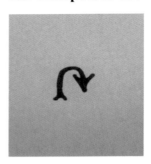

On October 15, 2015, Traverse City Area Public Schools (TCAPS) announced that three of its outlying schools with fewer than two hundred students each were causing an unbearable financial burden on the district. The schools—Bertha Vos IB School, Interlochen Community School, and Old Mission Elementary School—would be closed.

The residents of the Old Mission Peninsula, many alumni, and families with current or former students were stunned, but TCAPS was firm. The $400,000 overhead needed to keep the peninsula school open would instead be funneled to boost offerings in schools closer to the city.

With their historic passion for providing and maintaining quality education on the Old Mission Peninsula, the residents came together to save their school. A focus group that eventually included more than one hundred people began meeting on Saturday mornings at the Peninsula Community Library. Initially, the goal was to bring solutions to TCAPS that would lower the overhead required to keep the school open.

The focus group not only came up with options but also with money. Suggestions included developing unique programming, changing the start and finish times to attract families sending their children to city schools that dismissed in time for after-school activities, relocating the district's gifted and talented program to the Old Mission Elementary School, and going back to the original district lines. In addition, the group offered TCAPS $800,000 in exchange for keeping the school open for two years while it examined other options.

All suggested modifications were turned down although the $800,000 did pique interest. The TCAPS Board of Education gave the school a one-year extension to work on an offer and closed the Bertha Vos and Interlochen schools.

The 2016–'17 school year was an extremely busy and creative one on the Old Mission Peninsula. Donations to save the school continued to flow in, so much so that it was time to get serious about an idea that had been floating around: that of creating an educational foundation to raise and manage funds. On September 14, 2016, the Old Mission Peninsula Educational Foundation (OMPEF) was officially incorporated with the "mission of enhancing educational opportunities on Old Mission Peninsula."

During an August community meeting with the trustees, OMPEF decided to make an offer of one million dollars to TCAPS to purchase the school building, property, and non-proprietary contents. The offer was presented to the TCAPS board on November 14, 2016.

After months of negotiation, TCAPS accepted an offer of $1.1 million dollars for the school. In April of 2017, OMPEF took possession and the new school began to take shape. Old Mission Peninsula School, its former name restored, was to become a tuition-free charter school open to all residents of the Old Mission Peninsula and beyond. Grand Valley State University granted a charter to establish the new school in July of 2017.

The module-based El Education Curriculum created by the Harvard Graduate School of Education and Outward Bound was chosen whereby students would study specific subjects such as frogs or tools in depth for an eight- or nine-week period. Science, language arts, social studies, and engineering would be drawn into each module's topic of study. The program called Math in Focus, chosen to provide the mathematical component of the curriculum, would teach through both concrete and abstract experiences.

Superb educators and small class sizes were top priorities. Grades K–3 would be limited to fifteen students each and grades 4–6 to a maximum of twenty students each. Grades K–3 would each have two classrooms, and grades 4–6 would each have one classroom. Daycare, preschool, and before- and after-school care would also be provided. The staff would include eleven general education teachers and one special education teacher.

The new Old Mission Peninsula School opened its doors on September 4, 2018, a very rainy day. Although nature tried, she could not dampen the spirits of parents, students, or teachers.

Today, having completed its first year and begun its second, the school is thriving due to hard work and robust community support.

Looking to the future, Old Mission Peninsula School hopes to soon serve grades K–8 once again, cycling back to its beginning.

Ava, Mackey and Cooper Hartley completing their first year at Old Mission Peninsula School

References

EL Education Curriculum. curriculum.eleducation.org. About Us.

Manning, Craig. "A New Chapter Set to Begin at Old Mission School." *The Ticker*. August 13, 2018.

"Our History." Old Mission Peninsula Education Foundation. https://www.ompef.org/.

Chapter Ten

It Takes a Community

Bees. Children. Communities.

All learn. All grow. All change to survive and, better yet, thrive.

From its earliest days to the present, education remains vital to our survival. The need to pass on information pertinent to the society in which we live is paramount, but the manner in which we educate, and the information we pass on, has changed over time.

What our grandparents needed to know to survive and thrive is very different from the requirements of today. Over the years, the Old Mission Peninsula community has been very successful in its efforts to maintain high quality education for its students.

The key word is "community."

The belief that "It takes a community to raise a child" is practically a cliché, but, after all, clichés develop as they come to reflect accepted wisdom.

Support for community-focused education has been evident on the Old Mission Peninsula throughout time. The Native American community educated its children, the one-room schoolhouses defined community, consolidation redefined the community, and the community saved its school.

What will the future bring for the educational community on the Old Mission Peninsula? Only time will tell, but if the past is any indication, the sky is indeed the limit.

Old Mission Peninsula School in 2019.
Photo courtesy of Christopher Rieser.

Appendix

Timeline of Education on the Old Mission Peninsula

- 1741–1840: Odawa and Ojibwa tribal education

- 1840–1857: Peter Dougherty era

- Late 1800s: Clementina Holdsworth's home, McMullen's barn, the Hesler Log Cabin

- 1851–1852: the schooner *Madeline*

- 1857–1955: Old Mission School

- Around 1883–1893: Archie School

- 1859–1955: Stoney Beach School

- 1862–1955: McKinley School

- 1864–1955: Bowers Harbor School

- 1865–1955: Mapleton School

- 1884–1955: Ogdensburg School

- 1896–1958: Maple Grove School

- 1956: Old Mission Peninsula School (OMPS) is built after consolidation occurs

- 1968: OMPS is incorporated into Traverse City Area Public Schools (TCAPS) and becomes Old Mission Elementary School

- 2018: Old Mission Elementary School becomes a charter school and is once again called Old Mission Peninsula School

Made in the USA
Lexington, KY
04 December 2019

57998204R00031